Kindle Fire HD User's Guide 5th Generation Manual: Unleash the Power of Your Tablet!

By Shelby Johnson

Disclaimer:

This eBook is an unofficial guide for using the 2015 Kindle Fire HD and is not meant to replace any official documentation that came with the device. The information in this guide is meant as recommendations and suggestions, but the author bears no responsibility for any issues arising from improper use of the tablet. The owner of the device is responsible for taking all necessary precautions and measures with their tablet.

Kindle, Kindle Fire HD, and Amazon are trademarks of Amazon or its affiliates. All other trademarks are the property of their respective owners. The author and publishers of this book are not associated with any product or vendor mentioned in this book. Any Kindle Fire HD screenshots are meant for educational purposes only.

Author Introduction

Hi, I'm Shelby Johnson, a technology enthusiast, new Kindle Fire HD owner, and bestselling Amazon eBook author. With this newest tablet from Amazon, I absolutely love its many standard features and capabilities, but have found there is so much more that can be done with this amazing gadget than you may realize.

I've learned a lot of great things you can do with a Kindle Fire HD and want to help others get more out of their Kindle Fire HD devices. I have created this guide to be the best way to get the most out of your Kindle Fire HD. Without it, you may find yourself lost. At the very least, you will miss out on some of the amazing features this tablet offers that you do not know about.

This eBook is ESSENTIAL for any new Kindle Fire HD owner. If you give a Kindle Fire HD as a gift and do NOT purchase this guide, you're giving an incomplete gift.

Here is just some of the great info you'll find in this User's Guide Book:

How to use Second Screen.

How to create Collections.

How to set parental control limits for children using your tablet.

How to set up Household Profiles.

How to get Google Chrome or other web browsers on your Kindle device.

How to sideload android apps onto your Kindle Fire.

You'll learn all of the above and more in this book, which features screenshots from the Kindle and step-by-step instructions on the processes involved, so that you can unleash the many powerful features your Kindle device offers!

For a listing of the best Kindle accessories see the **Tech Media Source** website.

Table of Contents

Introduction

With the popularity of tablets firmly entrenched, Amazon has launched its fifth generation Kindle Fire. These newest generation tablets are the Kindle Fire and the Kindle Fire HD. These devices come in several versions, with a number of storage options for everyone from the novice, e-reader, and web surfer, to the professionally savvy social media moguls around the globe.

The Kindle Fire HD is available in a 6-inch, 8-inch or 10-inch screens, with multiple fun colors from which to choose, and some of the models have expandable storage up to 128GB using the onboard SD Card slot. With various options and pricing depending on the model, it is safe to say no matter which one suits your fancy, you will be ready to take on the world in high definition style from the moment it leaves the box.

This eBook is perfect for novices, intermediates, and advanced techies looking for how-tos with their new device. For those who aren't necessarily tech savvy, but received the Amazon tablet as a gift, it can be a bit daunting to try to figure everything out. This eBook will help you get to know your tablet even better, while fully unlocking and unleashing many of the extra capabilities the device possesses!

The Kindle Fire

The new Kindle Fire HD is chock full of technological genius that comes to life on a stunning that provides exceptional high definition color accuracy, reduced glare, and great pixel density.

The Kindle Fire HD adds to the quickness and display by boasting 8 hours of battery life, in an effort to keep you up to speed on everything in your world without compromising the duration of its use.

This ultra-light and incredibly durable device couples its speed and balance with amenities that include front and rear facing cameras, free cloud storage, instant video downloads and the fun of X-Ray for your music files, so you can follow along to the words onscreen, or learn more about the band as you enjoy their songs. What's more is that it can be activated for movies, so you can interact with trivia or catch up on the backstories of characters.

With hundreds of new features in the Fire OS 5 Bellini you can personalize your new Kindle Fire HD to match your every need, while it reflects your personality from the outside. Choose from different cases, screen protectors, keyboards, artwork and bedazzling effects as your personality dictates – or shuffle between several accordingly. This device is going to blow you away with its incredibly graphics and absolute functionality, so you are going to cozy up to it in no time, and want to care for it as if it will last a lifetime. As with all new and exciting devices, there is always more than meets the eye, so let's jump right into this device's offerings.

What's in the Box?

The Kindle Fire HD arrives packed neatly in its box.

Enclosed in the eco-friendly box is:

- The Kindle Fire HD tablet.
- One Page, two-sided "Getting to know your Kindle Fire HDX" Quick Card.
- Square-shaped Fast Wall Charger (USB port on the top, plugs directly into the wall).
- Micro-USB Charge & Sync Cable.

There is no hefty user guide, as the device works intuitively, and allows you to operate it functionally without confusion – or the fear that you have done something completely wrong. Should you become button happy, however, and find yourself stranded in technological limbo, help is just a tap away.

Getting to Know your Kindle

Once you open the KFHD you will notice how sleek it is, and that it sits flush on a hard surface, so there is no rocking involved in its use, if you plan to sit it down instead of hold it. The power button and the volume button are both on the top of the 2015 Kindle Fire HD. If you can read the word "Amazon," which appears on the back of the tablet, correctly from left to right, than the power button will be at the top right-hand of the KFHD, and the volume buttons will be at the top left-hand (assuming you are holding it with two hands!)

There are two Dolby speakers on the left side of the device, which are identified by their slatted design. On the very same side of the device as the volume control you will find a 3.5mm stereo jack port for headphones.

In addition, a micro-USB connection is located next to the power button, which is how you will power your KFHD, and connect it to another source for data transfers when necessary.

With the 2015 Kindle Fire HD Amazon has reintroduced the MicroSD card storage slot option! This is good news to many Kindle owners. The slot is located on the upper right-hand side of the tablet (not on the top where the power buttons are, but the side). Later in this guide we'll discuss how to insert and use the optional additional storage.

Getting Started with your Kindle Fire HD

The good news regarding your device is that is arrives with approximately 65% of its battery power intact, so you can start setting it up right away. When you are ready to charge it, simply plug the micro-USB cable into the device, and directly into the wall charger, before plugging the charger itself into the wall.

Because you should have more than enough battery power to get going, set aside a few minutes to set up your device's initial preferences, so you can start using it right away! Once you have completed the set-up, allow it to charge to 100% so you can test the battery life out for yourself. Although the device boasts 8 hours of use, it will differ for everyone. Also, it may take a week or two to start using it at a regular pace. Usually, when someone receives a new device, the battery will not last nearly as long as possible, because they are constantly using it in different capacities to learn the device's capabilities through and through.

Setting up the KFHD

Once you turn the device on, you are going to be ready to start setting it up with your personal framework and preferences, so you can enjoy its beauty without delay in a very personalized way. The first thing you will notice is that even when the device is locked the time (which is not correct yet, unless you got really lucky somehow!) and battery life with an icon and the actual percentage on display immediately.

Turning on KFHD

The first thing you will do is turn on your new Kindle Fire HD. Simply press and hold the button on the top right of the device. Your Kindle will power on. First Amazon will display across the screen and then that will change to Fire.

Choosing Language

Once you've turned on your device, you will be asked to pick a language. Currently the following options are available, and can be changed under your settings tab (more on this later!) should you (or someone else) accidentally change it – or set it up in a native tongue other than yours.

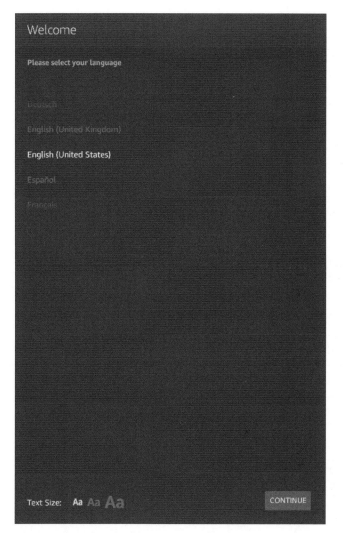

Choose your language and click the continue button.

Connecting to Wireless Network

Your device will identify the closest Wi-Fi network, and will require you to enter the password – assuming it is password protected (a lock symbol next to the router's name will tell you so).

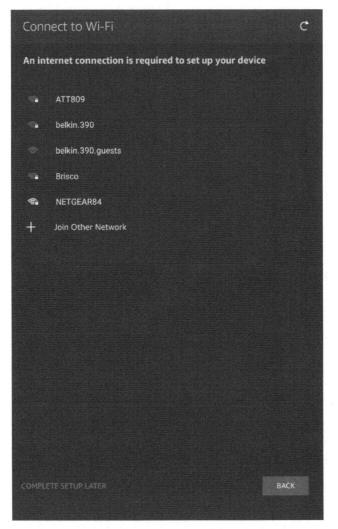

Once you connect to a wireless network, the latest Fire software will install on the device. It will take a few minutes, and the device will automatically restart.

Note: *Make sure you have enough battery charge to complete the software update.*

Registering Kindle

After your Kindle Fire HD software has updated to the latest version, the device will restart, and it will immediately ask you to register your KFHD using your Amazon account username and password.

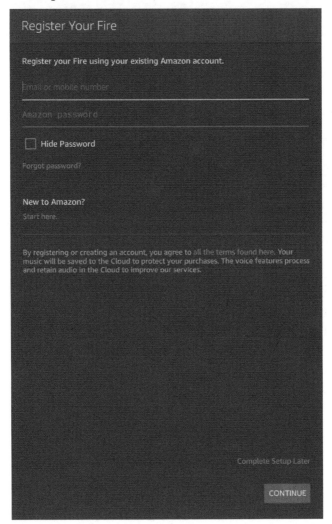

Note: *If you do not have an Amazon account, you can tap "Start here" under "New to Amazon?" and follow the onscreen instructions to create one. It will also automatically set the time for you, based on the router's current time.*

Confirm your Time Zone

Once you connect to your Wi-Fi, the Kindle Fire HD will detect the time zone used by the Wi-Fi network. If the time zone is incorrect, press "Time zone incorrect?" and follow the instructions. If the time zone is correct, simply press the continue button.

Family Setup

You can set up your Kindle Fire HD to share with your family. If you would rather not, you can also just set it up for yourself. In this section, you can set up child profiles to include on your device.

Note: Each KFHD can have two adult profiles, and the second profile can be set in the Profiles and Family Library setting area.

Child Profile Setup

To set up Child Profiles complete the following steps:

1. Tap the circle next to Yes, and press the continue button.
2. Type in a name for the profile.

3. Choose gender and birthday.
4. Choose either to Use FreeTime for the profile if child is under 11 or Use Teen Profiles and Family Library for children 11 and older.
5. Click "Create Profile."
6. Next you can either press "Add another child" or press Continue.

Set Lock Screen PIN

If you created a child profile, you will need to set a lock screen PIN. The PIN must consist of 4 characters.

1. Choose a PIN and inter it into the space.
2. Confirm PIN.
3. Press Finish.

Note: *You can hide profiles by going to Profiles & Family Library in the Settings. After that, you can turn off the lock screen PIN by going to Settings, then Security.*

Enable Location Services

You can choose to enable location services to allow Maps and other apps to use your location related information to improve your user experience. Simply press "No Thanks" or "Enable."

Note: *Location Services may use more battery power.*

Backup & Auto-Save

In this section of your device setup, you can choose to Backup and Restore your device settings, Save Wi-Fi Passwords to Amazon, and Auto-Save your Photos and Videos to the Amazon Cloud Drive.

Simply move the slider on the right-hand to the right to turn on the selected features and press "Continue." If you would rather not set up any of these features, you can choose "No Thanks" at the bottom of the screen.

Connect Social Networks

You can connect to Twitter, Facebook, and Goodreads using this screen. To connect to any of these social networks, choose the social network, and then enter your username and login information. Once you have connected to as many or as few as you would like, press "Continue" at the bottom of the page.

Protect your Fire

On this screen Amazon offers you the opportunity to buy a 2-Year Protection plan if you haven't already purchased it. Simply choose "Purchase for $29.99" if you want the plan, or choose "No thanks, continue without protection."

Note: The protection plan is completely optional.

Congratulations! You have completed the initial setup of your new Kindle Fire HD tablet. Now you can choose to take the Welcome tutorial to guide you through the tablet's functionality, or you can explore on your own. To take the tutorial press "Start." To exit, press "Exit."

In the next section, you will learn how to navigate your new device.

Navigating the Kindle Fire

Chances are that by now you are pretty enamored with the screen's display; it is a thing of beauty. So as you begin to use your Kindle Fire HD, there are a few tips to the navigation. Feel free to bounce around for a while to see which swiping motions and views work best for you. Remember, everyone has a different idea of what works for them technologically, and this device gives you the opportunity to embrace your personal approach to organization.

Also, along the top of your screen you will see the following options as you swipe to the right:

- Search
- Recent
- Home
- Books
- Video
- Games
- Shop
- Apps
- Music
- Audiobooks
- Newstand

Inside these sections, you can view available content within them like eBooks, music lists or movies without returning to the home screen. This is a great way to remain focused in the category you are in, instead of jumping back and forth from home to music (or movies, or otherwise).

Options Bar

Within any screen – other than the home screen – you can access the options bar, which allows you to go back to the previous page by pressing a back arrow, see your open taps by pressing the square icon, and the ability to get to the home screen by tapping the circle icon.

There is one more icon, which is comprised of three lines. This is the menu icon, and will provide various functions and settings; depending on which content library you are in (not pictured in the above screenshot).

Notifications and Quick Settings

When you swipe down from the top of your Kindle Fire HD, you will see recent notifications, and above that, there is a quick settings menu.

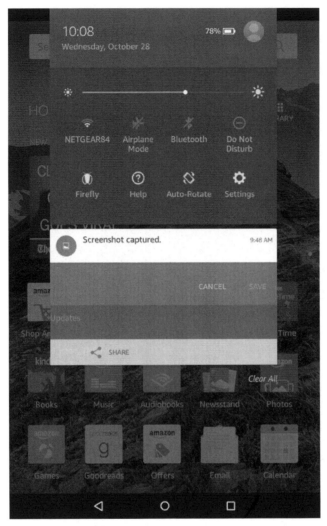

In this quick settings menu you can adjust the screen's brightness, turn Wi-Fi on or off, turn Airplane Mode on or off, turn Bluetooth on or off, turn Do Not Disturb on or off, access the Camera, access Help, turn Auto-Rotate on or off, and access the device Settings.

To clear your recent notifications, push "Clear All" and "No Notifications" will appear. To return to the Home Screen, press the circle button.

How to use the Kindle Fire HD

There are many things you will want to know how to do with your new Kindle Fire device. The following sections give detailed answers to your most comment "how to" questions.

How to Set Up Email

You can set up your email account – or a number of email addresses – directly on the device, so that you can keep in touch with friends, family, or even the office. The ease lies in the fact that there is an actual email app on the Kindle Fire HD, so you can easily set up all of your important email accounts including Gmail, Yahoo! AOL and Outlook, just to name a few.

Simply tap on the Email App Icon, and enter the email address of the account you want to add, and your password. Tap continue and allow it a few seconds to set up automatically. Repeat the process for each of the accounts you would like to add.

1. From the home screen, tap the "Email" app.
2. Enter your e-mail address, and then tap "Next."
3. Enter the password for your e-mail account, and then tap "Next."

4. If your e-mail account is not recognized, tap "Advanced Setup" to manually add your e-mail account to your Kindle Fire HD.

Change, add or delete email accounts at any time by using the steps listed above. There is no limit to the amount of accounts you can add, and each one will allow you to access them in their entirety including email threads, drafts, trash and complete folders. You will also be given the option to delete the email on your phone, but save it on your work computer, just so you do not miss a beat – or inadvertently overlook something.

How to Set up Calendar

When you are ready to manage your meetings, events, and day-to-day schedule with the Calendar App, you have a number of options to choose from so all of your happenings are listed in one place. You can sync Gmail, Yahoo! Mail, Exchange, Outlook, Hotmail, and Facebook calendars to your Kindle Fire HD. Also, you can sync your calendar among all your Amazon devices.

The app will open to the current date, and you will see any appointments or entries you have put into the calendar.

1. From the Home Screen, tap the "Calendar" app.
2. Tap the 3 vertical dots on the right-hand corner to see Agenda, Day, Week, Month, or Refresh.
3. Tap the 3 horizontal lines on the left to open the Settings, Add account or Help sections.

To add a new event, complete the following steps:

1. Tap the "plus" sign at the bottom right of the screen.
2. Enter a Title.

3. Adjust the Start and End times or choose All Day
4. Choose how often or if this event Repeats on your calendar.
5. Choose "Remind me" and set when you would like to be reminded.
6. Choose account.
7. Add a location if you would like to.
8. Add a note.
9. Press the "check mark" in the top right-hand corner to add the event.

Once you are inside of the application you can change the calendar view to reveal the day, week, month or even lists you have created. You can also view or hide calendars just by swiping from the left side of the screen and tapping on any calendar that is synced with your Kindle. You can also view, create or edit and delete events you have created at any time

Connecting Facebook, Twitter and Goodreads

If you currently have a Facebook account all you have to do is enter your username and password to continue. The same goes for Twitter and Goodreads. If you already have an account, simply enter your username and password and tap continue to be taken directly to your account.

If you do not have social media accounts, you can skip the process altogether, or set up an account at another time (or right then, if you prefer!). You can also setup one and not the other, if you have a preference, so there is no need to get a Facebook page just to honor the device's available options, if you are more of a Twitter person.

Should you decide to skip the setup and come back to it, simply do the following:

1. Swipe the screen downward from the top.
2. Tap "Settings."
3. Tap "My Account."
4. Tap "Social Network" (choose Facebook, Twitter or Goodreads).
5. Enter the account information and tap "Done."

You can unlink your Facebook or Twitter account at any time going forward, and simply tap on their app icons to access your page directly whenever you would like.

How to Deregister Your Kindle

If your Kindle Fire HD was a gift, or you purchased it with the help of a friend's account, you'll want to make sure it is not registered to them once you start making purchases with it. To deregister a Kindle Fire HD, complete the following steps.

1. Swipe down from the top of the screen, and select "Settings" from the menu.
2. Choose "My Account" under the "Personal" heading.
3. Choose "Deregister" the device.

You can also deregister your device another way.

1. Logon to Amazon.com
2. Visit the "Manage Your Kindle" page. You will see the option to deregister the device at any time. This is also important to remember if you ever decide to give away or sell your Kindle Fire HD to someone else since you won't want them making purchases on your Amazon account.

How to Change Your Kindle Name

You may want to change the name of your new Kindle Fire HD. There are a couple of ways to do this. The easiest way is right on the device.

1. Swipe down from the top of the screen, and select "Settings" from the menu.
2. Choose "Device Options" under the "Device" heading.
3. Choose "Change Your Device Name" and type in the new name in the box that pops up.
4. Select save.

If you do not have your device with you, but you want to change its name, you can also do it online.

1. Log in to your Amazon.com account on your computer or Kindle device.
2. Go to the "Your Account" drop down menu and choose "Manage Your Kindle."
3. On the left side of the menu chooses under "Your Kindle Account" choose "Manage Your Devices."
4. In this section you'll see all registered Kindles for your account. You'll see the name of your Kindle Fire HD, which you can click "Edit" next to and change the name of your device.

Note: *In this section you can also choose to opt out of sponsored ads (for a $15 charge) and Register or Deregister your Kindle device.*

How to set up 1-Click Payment Option and adding Gift Cards & Codes

The 1-Click payment option will be your payment method for purchasing content on your Kindle Fire HD.

1. Swipe down and select "Settings."
2. Choose "My Account" under the "Personal" heading.
3. Choose "Amazon Account Settings."
4. Choose "Payment Options."
5. Choose 1-Click Payment Method and sign into your Amazon account. Select Continue.
6. Edit your Default Billing Method to the card you want to use for 1-Click Payment.

You may have a gift card or special code you want to redeem using your new Kindle Fire HD. If so, complete the following:

1. Swipe down and select "Settings."
2. Choose "My Account" under the "Personal" heading.
3. Choose "Amazon Account Settings."

4. Choose "Payment Options."
5. Choose "Gift Cards & Promotion Codes."
6. Add the code, and select "Apply to Your Account."

Note: *You can also see your current gift card or promotional code balance in this area as well as view your recent purchase activity.*

How to Adjust Kindle Fire HD Settings

With the amount of settings on any electronic device, it is easy to get confused about which option does what. The following explanations should help clear up any confusion going forward, so your device is used optimally at all times.

To access the various settings for your Kindle, hold down on the clock/time area at the top middle of your Kindle Fire HD screen, and then drag it down. You will reveal options such as "Brightness," "Wireless," "Airplane Mode," "Bluetooth," "Do Not Disturb," "Camera," "Help," "Auto-Rotate," and "Settings."

Brightness

Tapping the orange line above the buttons will adjust the screen brightness. Slide it left or right to reduce or increase the brightness of your screen.

Wireless

This is where you will see any available Wireless network(s). Select the network you want to connect to, and type in the user name and password to connect.

Airplane Mode

The term "Airplane Mode" is derived from the ability to use your mobile electronic device without causing interference to other electronic signals around you. Simply put, when your Kindle Fire HD is in Airplane Mode, your ability to use the Internet or Bluetooth is shut off. This is best used as one would guess, when traveling by airplane.

This means you can still use your Kindle Fire HD to read eBooks or documents, play games, listen to music, watch movies or use the camera of the device without interrupting the signal transmissions around you — say, on an airplane. This makes the device safe to use when it typically would not be permitted due to the possibility of signal interference. All of your activities on the device will be done offline, with Wi-Fi and Bluetooth inactive. If the plane you are traveling on offers Wi-Fi service, then you may be able to switch Airplane Mode off and use your tablet as you normally would.

Bluetooth

Bluetooth is an open wireless technology that exchanges data over short distances, using radio transmissions. It operates from a fixed or mobile device, in this case your Kindle Fire HD, to create a personal area network.

When Bluetooth is enabled on your device, you will see a small Bluetooth symbol up on the top area of your display, near your Wi-Fi symbol and battery status indicator.

This technology can be used for phones and wireless headsets or intercoms. In the case of the Kindle Fire HD, it can be connected to a wireless mouse, keyboard or printer. It can also allow movies and music to be played on wireless devices such as speakers or television screens with Bluetooth enabled technology.

One example of a way Bluetooth can be used is to transfer files such as pictures, music or videos from a smartphone to your Kindle Fire HD. To do this, the devices will need to be "paired" with one another. You must have a compatible device in order to do this that has Bluetooth connectivity. There are many smartphones, laptops, computers, and handheld devices that have Bluetooth capability.

When you tap the "Bluetooth" icon you will be able to pair available Bluetooth devices for use with your KFHD.

Do Not Disturb

When you tap the "Do Not Disturb" icon, it turns white. Using this feature allows you to perform tasks like reading an eBook without the interference of bothersome notifications.

When you want your device to go completely quiet, simply press the button, and you will not receive notifications that will disrupt you. To resume regular functionality, simply press the "Do Not Disturb" icon again and it will no longer be white. Notifications will resume as usual.

Firefly

Amazon Firefly uses your camera and microphone to help you gather information you want to know about movies, music, books, products, and even business cards among other things. To start using Firefly, click on the icon, and a new screen will open.

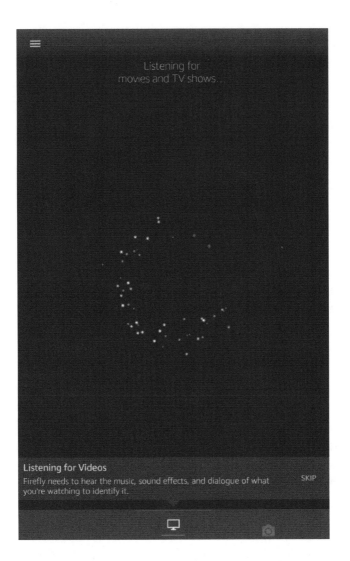

Packaged Products

Firefly identifies packaged products by using the size, shape, graphics, and details, or you can scan the barcode. You can find out how much an item costs and even get customer ratings.

Music

Firefly will help you figure out who sings the song. In addition, Firefly will provide the song's lyrics, biography of the artist, a music video, and the music's available formats.

Movies and TV Shows

Firefly can recognize TV shows and movies when you allow it to listen. Firefly can tell you the name of the show or movie you're watching as well as give you a list of the actors in the current scene.

Books

Firefly uses a book's cover to get ratings, review, and pricing along with availability. Who said you can't judge a book by its cover?

Phone Numbers, Emails, Text, and More

Firefly will recognize business cards. It will read phone numbers, email addresses, URLs from them. Firefly can also read QR codes and get this information.

Wines

Firefly will read wine labels from the bottle and provide ratings, reviews, price, and local availability. Firefly will even suggest food pairings for the wine!

Famous Paintings

Are you looking at a painting and can't remember who painted it? Firefly can help. The service can recognize thousands of famous paintings from around the world.

Help

Tap the "Help" icon to get answers to your questions. Specifically you can find help videos, a tutorial for Fire OS 5, a User Guide, help for Wireless connections, plus contact information for Amazon by email and phone.

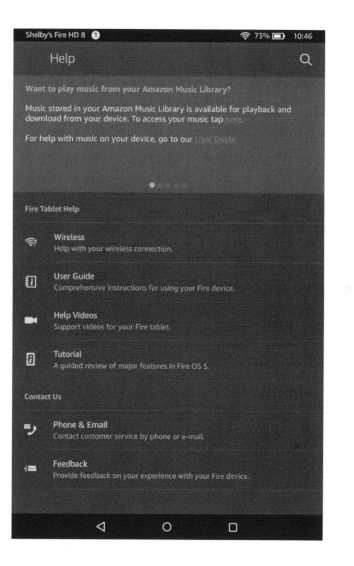

Shelby's Fire HD 8 ❶   73% 🔋 10:46

Help   🔍

Want to play music from your Amazon Music Library?

Music stored in your Amazon Music Library is available for playback and download from your device. To access your music tap here.

For help with music on your device, go to our User Guide

Fire Tablet Help

Wireless
Help with your wireless connection.

User Guide
Comprehensive instructions for using your Fire device.

Help Videos
Support videos for your Fire tablet.

Tutorial
A guided review of major features in Fire OS 5.

Contact Us

Phone & Email
Contact customer service by phone or e-mail.

Feedback
Provide feedback on your experience with your Fire device.

Auto-Rotate

The Auto-Rotate feature is incredibly simple to use. Simply tap the "Auto-Rotate" button to turn the feature on or off. When it is on, your Kindle's screen will not automatically rotate when you change the device's orientation. When it is off, your Kindle's screen will rotate when you reorient the device.

Settings

By pressing the "Settings" icon, you can access the Settings menu for your KFHD. Below are the settings available for the Kindle Fire HD when you tap on the "Settings" icon.

Device

- Wireless
- Storage
- Power
- Apps & Games
- Display
- Device Options

Personal

- My Account
- Profiles & Family Library
- Parental Controls
- Security
- Sound & Notification

- Keyboard & Language

System

- Sync Device
- Help
- Accessibility
- Legal & Compliance

To change the settings in any area of your Kindle Fire HD, access this Settings menu and choose the area where you want to make changes.

How to Set Security Options for Your Kindle Fire

Among the settings on your device is "Security." This setting is particularly helpful for protecting your device from unauthorized use and safeguarding any important data you have on the device. One of the best things you can do is to "Lock Screen Passcode" as described next.

← Security

Lock Screen

Lock Screen Passcode
Use a PIN/Password to protect the data on your Fire.

Advanced

Apps from Unknown Sources
Allow installation of applications that are not from Appstore.

Credential Storage
View and store digital certificates that are typically used for VPN and enterprise Wi-Fi access.

Device Administrators
See which applications are authorized as device administrators for your Fire.

You can use this option to set up a password for your Kindle Fire HD. This way when the device is locked and someone goes to unlock it, they will need to enter your PIN # to use the device. This is helpful to protect your device in the event it is misplaced or stolen, so that any vital data is not stolen. To set up a Lock Screen Password, touch this selection on the screen, and then enter a PIN # of at least 4 characters. Make sure it is a number you will remember, but not one a stranger would easily guess.

The VPN option will allow you to use the Kindle in a virtual private network, or VPN. To do this you will need to download a special app from the Amazon Appstore. This is a more complex setup that may require the help of an IT professional from your office, or someone in your home with knowledge of your network.

You can also set "Device Administrators" in the Security area. This will allow multiple users to be in charge of the Kindle Fire HD, such as a set of parents, teachers, or others. It can be helpful for keeping the device protected from unauthorized use by children, for example.

How to set up Household Profiles

You can share your Kindle Fire HD with your entire household. However, each user can have his or her own profile. The Kindle Fire HD allows you to set up one additional adult profile for a total of two adult profiles as well as multiple child profiles.

It should be noted that profiles for other adults in the household require a unique Amazon account for each adult. You can use Family Library to access content from the main device account.

1. Swipe down and select "Settings."
2. Select "Profiles & Family Library" under the Personal heading.
3. Choose "Add a second adult profile" or "Add a child profile."
4. Follow on screen instructions for adding either type of profile.
   Note: the section below gives more details and instructions for setting up Parental controls on child profiles.

How to set up Kindle Fire HD Parental Controls

As any parent is aware, technology can easily take over your child's ability to interact with others, or to even do their homework, if certain boundaries are not established. Even when they are understood, if you happen to be out of sight, or away from the house, the boundaries may be overlooked to steal away a few extra minutes of Internet surfing. That is why the Kindle Fire HD provides Parental Controls that allow you to establish time limits for certain users, while enabling content controls for curious eyes.

Kindle Fire HD provides parents with all the tools they need to police their child's device usage. In fact, it even comes with its very own name: FreeTime. This service is available for children 10 and under and you can use a teen profile for kids 11 and up.

To turn on Parental Controls complete the following steps:

1. Swipe down and select "Settings."
2. Select "Parental Controls" under the Personal heading.
3. Turn Parental Controls on by moving slider to the right.
4. Enter a new password, confirm and press finish.
5. Choose activities to block or unblock, choose to password protect purchases and video playback as well as Wi-Fi and Location Services.

You will be met with a bevy of options to control with your device including web browsing, e-mail, contacts, and calendars. In addition, and more importantly, you can password protect purchases, videos, content, and Wi-Fi connections.

← **Parental Controls**

Household Profiles
You can add an adult and up to 4 children on this device. For children 17 and under, you can create a profile and choose content you have purchased for each child. You have complete control over which content each child can access.

Parental Controls
Restrict purchasing, content types, web browsing and access to other features

Web Browser — Blocked

Email, Contacts, Calendars — Blocked

Social Sharing — Blocked

Camera — Blocked

Amazon Maps — Unblocked

Firefly — Unblocked

Amazon Stores
To restrict Amazon Instant Video, use Password Protect Video Playback — Unblocked

Password Protect Purchases
Require a password to purchase and download from the Amazon Stores or the Shop Amazon app

Password Protect Video Playback
Require a password to play Video

You can also set time limits for games and content, but can give your child unlimited access to books or educational material, which cannot be changed by anyone but you (or another adult with the password). Separate profiles can be set up for multiple children, with each only having access to the material you, as the parent, establish as safe and relevant to their age and lifestyle. This will create a fun, safe and easy-to-use environment for younger Kindle Fire HD users.

To create child profiles complete the following steps:

5. Swipe down and select "Settings."
6. Select "Parental Controls" under the Personal heading.
7. Choose "Household Profiles."
8. Choose "Add a child profile."
9. Set a PIN, confirm, and select "Finish."
10. Input name, gender and birthday.
11. Choose Amazon FreeTime for kids 10 and younger or Teen Profiles for kids 11 and older.
12. Select "Add Profile."
13. Repeat instructions to add additional child profiles.

Exit Child Profiles or Change Settings from Inside

To exit Child Profiles or change settings from within an app, book or other piece of content, you'll need to tap on the screen near the top to drag down the notifications menu bar. Choose "Exit" or the option you want to control, and enter your password.

Kindle Fire HD How Tos

The following sections give many Kindle Fire HD how tos. Some of these you won't find in the regular user's manual.

How to Pair a Bluetooth Device with Kindle Fire HD

The KFHD comes equipped with Bluetooth, which means you may have many devices you can use with your tablet. However, before you can use a device, you must pair it with the tablet. The following instructions explain how to pair a Bluetooth Device with your KFHD tablet.

1. Swipe down from the top of the screen to reveal the notifications menu at the top of your display.
2. Tap on "Bluetooth."
3. Turn Bluetooth on by moving slider to the right. It will turn orange, and say "Your Fire is now Discoverable."
4. The Kindle Fire HD will search for any devices in the region with Bluetooth connectivity turned on. It may take several minutes to find some devices.
5. Tap on the device that you want to pair to begin the pairing process.
6. You will receive a pop-up box on your computer or other device, as well as a pop-up box on the Kindle Fire HD explaining how to complete the pairing process. Generally, this involves checking both devices to make sure a numerical code matches on them. In some cases, you will need to type the code in for one of the devices.
7. Once paired, you can use your computer or other device to send files via Bluetooth to the Kindle Fire HD, as long as both

devices remain powered on and the Bluetooth connectivity remains on as well. Some examples of devices that I've personally used this with successfully are LG smartphones and a Mac Mini computer, but there are many other items out there that work.

8. Some of the files you can send via Bluetooth to your Kindle Fire HD include MP3's, documents, photos and videos. Once they have been sent to your Kindle Fire HD, they'll show up in the notifications area or in the appropriate section of your Kindle Fire HD device (i.e. photos, music, docs, etc.).

Note: *Keep in mind that some devices may show up on the Kindle Fire HD, but might not be Bluetooth compatible. For example, the Apple iPhone 5 is among the non-compatible devices. Also, pairing a keyboard or headset will require a different process as described in that device's instructions.*

How to Purchase Content for Kindle Fire HD

You can purchase content, including music, movies, books, magazines and television programming through your device. Remember, you will have to have your One-click purchasing account set up before you do so, but that takes only a few seconds,

To make purchases tap on any of the various types of content (i.e. Games, Apps, Books, Music, Videos). Tapping on these choices will bring up whatever content you currently have stored on your device and in the cloud. It will also have a "Store" option you can tap on to start shopping for more content.

In addition to purchasing items that will exist on your tablet, you can purchase ANYTHING that is available at Amazon.com. If you would like to buy a sweater for your mother for her birthday, simply browse the available selection, purchase the item, and ship it to her directly! Do you want to buy a bicycle for your son or daughter's birthday? Find the one you want at Amazon, and purchase it with one click. Their inventory of goods and technology is endless, and so is your ability to purchase them using your tablet.

How to Subscribe to Amazon Prime Service

Subscribing to the Amazon Prime Service is easy, affordable, and provides members with an endless amount of perks, simply for signing up and paying the annual fee. Amazon members can go sign-up now for a one-month free trial to start enjoying unlimited instant streaming of thousands of movies and television shows, thanks to Prime Instant Videos. In addition, you will receive one free eBook borrowing opportunity each month from the Kindle Owners' Lending Library.

Also, going forward, you will receive free two day shipping on virtually every item you order from Amazon, with no minimum order size! After the first free month, the subscription is available for $99 per year, which will pay for itself in no time.

Many Kindle Fire HD owners and Amazon members opt for this service not only for the shipping, but also as an alternative to subscribing to Netflix for their streaming movies and TV shows, due to the wide selection of content Amazon offers.

How to Subscribe to Kindle Unlimited

If you read a lot of books on your Kindle Fire HD, then you might want to consider subscribing to **Kindle Unlimited** through Amazon. The subscription allows you access to hundreds of thousands of Kindle books and thousands of audiobooks with Whispersync for Voice. Subscribers can keep up to ten books at a time and there are no due dates.

This makes it easy to read as many books as you want in a month without worrying about busting your budget. For voracious readers, KU makes good sense.

How to Transfer Files via USB on a PC

You can transfer photos, music, documents, video, and many other file types from your computer to your Kindle Fire HD, and vice versa. You'll need to connect the included USB cable from your Kindle Fire HD to your computer first.

For PC's it should automatically connect your Kindle Fire HD to your computer and it will show up as a drive you can open. Once you've done that, you can simply drag and drop files from your computer to the Kindle Fire HD, and vice versa.

How to Transfer Files via USB on a MAC

For a MAC computer, you'll need to use the free Android File Transfer app to complete USB transfers. Go to Android File Transfer App in your computer browser and follow the onscreen instructions to download this utility.

Once you have it installed you can connect your Kindle Fire HD via the USB cable to your MAC. The Android File Transfer utility will show as a drive on your computer, similar to any other USB drive you might plug in. Once you are able to connect your Kindle Fire HD to your computer, you can drag and drop files between your Kindle and MAC computer. Make sure to click on the eject button next to the Android File Transfer drive on your MAC before unplugging the USB cable, just to be safe.

How to Listen to the Radio on Your Kindle

Did you know it is possible to stream local and national radio stations on your Kindle Fire HD? There is a great app called Tune In Radio, which is free at the Amazon Appstore. With this app you can listen to a wide range of local radio stations over your wireless connection. Additionally, you can choose from different categories including music, sports, news, talk and podcasts. The radio app will play as you use various features on your Kindle Fire HD making it a great way to enjoy music while using the tablet device.

How to Choose a Kindle Fire HD Web Browser

The Kindle Fire HD comes standard with the Amazon Silk browser, and the verdict is still out from most users as to whether this is the best option for your tablet. There are a few alternate browsers you might consider such as Dolphin Browser, or Google Chrome, which you may find to offer a more appealing and comfortable web browsing experience.

Dolphin Browser vs. Amazon Silk

Dolphin Browser is a quick moving, smart and free web-based browser that delivers stunning graphics, combined with impeccable search results, and will allow you to open your favorite pages with the tap of your fingers. PC Magazine calls Dolphin the most capable browser available for your tablet, and over 50 million downloaders could not agree more. Many Kindle Fire owners opt for this browser to help with resizing webpages to their liking for easier display and readability.

Amazon's Silk browser comes standard with the device. It basically chooses between two web browsing research options, with one of them being Amazon's servers. This means the information provided might be centered on Amazon's recommendations, instead of fully disclosed results.

Many users decide to install the Dolphin Browser, giving them another option to browse the Internet and better use the capabilities of the World Wide Web on their tablet. The biggest pro to obtaining the browser is it will allow for the use of Adobe Flash, which is a valuable component of many website. Adobe Flash support on the Dolphin browser allows for viewing of website video content on your Fire HD.

How to Install the Dolphin Browser

To install the Dolphin Browser, you must enable apps from unknown sources.

1. Go to "Settings."
2. Under the Personal heading choose "Security."
3. Choose "Apps from Unknown Sources" under the Advanced menu. Bypass the warning message on the popup box by tapping "OK" to enable this setting.

Once you have enabled apps from unknown sources, you are ready to finish

1. On your Kindle Fire HD, go to "Web" and then search for "Dolphin Browser HD 8.5.1."
2. Use the site you found, or you can try the one located at the **XDA-Developers forum**. (Remember, you are using these sites and links at your own risk.)
3. Download the "APK" file for 8.5.1 you find at the website.
4. Access your Notifications. Find the recent download. Tap on it to install.

Now you have the Dolphin Browser as an alternate web browser with many other settings you can set up.

How to Install Google Chrome Browser

Another web browser that some users might prefer to have on their Kindle Fire HD is Google Chrome. Here's how to install the Google Chrome browser on a Kindle Fire HD. (**Note:** *This involves "sideloading" an app which is only legal when you already own the app files yourself, for example from purchasing/downloading the app for your phone or other device*)

1. Pull down the notifications/setting bar at the top of your display (tap where the clock time shows at the top middle of screen and drag down).
2. Go to "More," then "Device," then tap "On" for "Allow Installation of Applications," if it is not already on.
3. A warning box will pop up. Tap on "OK" to bypass the warning box.
4. On your Kindle Fire HD or HDX, go to the web browser and do a search for the following file "com.android-chrome-2-apk" (without quotes). There will be various forums and websites that are hosting

this file. Be cautious as some sites may have spammy links or malware, but for the most part, forums such as the **XDA Developers forum** have been generally reliable for downloads of .apk files.

5. Download the file mentioned above to your Kindle. You will do this at the forum link above by tapping on the link provided. The file will start to automatically download.

6. Once the download has completed go back to your Home screen, drag down the notifications bar and tap on the recently downloaded .apk file.

7. You'll be asked, "Do you want to install this application?" Tap on "Install" at the bottom right area of the screen. This will install Chrome Beta on your Kindle Fire HD.

8. Once the installation is complete, tap on "Open" on the bottom of the screen.

9. You will now be able to use Google Chrome as an alternate browser on your Kindle Fire HD. Once you first open it, you may be prompted to accept a user agreement, as well as sign in to your Google account. Signing into a Google account is not required to use the browser.

Note: *You may experience difficulty trying to view YouTube videos on the YouTube website with Chrome browser on your Kindle Fire HD.*

How to Watch Movies on Your Kindle Fire HD

The Kindle Fire HD is a great device for entertainment, as it connects you to the vast selection of movies available for rental and purchase from the Amazon website. You can choose a new or older movie or TV show to watch, purchase it, and it will stream to your Kindle Fire HD tablet.

You'll be able to watch movies, TV shows, play games, use apps, and even browse the web on an even bigger and more vivid display, unleashing the Dolby sound and Hi-definition features!

How to Watch .WMV & .MOV Files on Your Kindle

Both .wmv and .mov files are a popular format for movies and videos. If you add them to your device, they will not show up on your device in the "Videos" Library. However, using the ES File Explorer app, you can view these videos on your device.

Once the app is installed, connect your Kindle Fire HD via the micro USB to your laptop. Simply drag the .wmv file(s) from your computer files over to your Kindle Fire HD's folders.

You can now open up ES File Explorer app on your tablet, and then find the .wmv file you want to view. Tap on it, and the video will begin to play on your tablet.

Note: For .mov files, you will be able to do the same as above, but you may receive a pop-up prompt asking what you want to view the video with. Tap on "ES Media Player." You might also want to tap on the checkbox "Set as the default app" before you do.

How to Use a Google Chromecast to Stream Video

The Google Chromecast ($35 at time of this publication) is another option for streaming video content to your TV. Chromecast is a "dongle" which Google released that you can plug into an HDMI spot on your TV for streaming content. Video content can be streamed from Netflix, Hulu Plus, YouTube, and in the case of some devices, anything from a Google Chrome web browser tab. While the device doesn't come compatible with the Kindle Fire HD, it can be worked around through sideloading to enable it to stream content from certain apps. *(Keep in mind, .apk file sideloading is considered illegal, unless they are files you have purchased and own for an Android device.)*

1. Install the free Hulu Plus app from the Amazon app store.
2. Install a Google Chromecast app apk file (do this by adding the .apk file to your Kindle's files and then open it with File Explorer app).
3. Install YouTube for Kindle Fire HD.

The Kindle Fire HD was tested to see if it would work with the Chromecast, and if you have the .apk files listed above, you can add them to your Kindle Fire HD folders and file directory. Once they're on the tablet, use something like the free ES File Explorer app to open the .apk files and install them.

Open the Chromecast app from inside ES File Explorer after you've installed. Go through the set up process to discover your Chromecast on your wireless network and make sure your Kindle Fire HD discovers it.

Launch the Hulu Plus app, or either of the other two apps mentioned above, and you'll see the Chromecast "symbol" on the video content you play on your tablet. Tap on that symbol and you can wirelessly stream to your Chromecast from the KFHD. The same should work for the sideloaded YouTube app.

As of this publication, this method was tested with Hulu Plus and YouTube apps. It worked well in both situations, and has yet to be tested with Netflix apps of any type. Chromecast streaming did not work with the Amazon Instant video content that was tested.

Amazon Prime vs. HuluPlus vs. Netflix

While there are thousands of movies at Amazon you can buy or rent, there is also the aforementioned Amazon Prime service. If you have this subscription based service, you can choose from any movies or shows listed in the Prime Instant Video area and watch them completely free of charge!

There are other options for watching movies or TV shows, two of which come from the subscription-based apps Netflix and HuluPlus, mentioned later on.

As of this report, Amazon Prime is $79 a year, with the first month free for anyone who buys a new Kindle Fire HD. HuluPlus costs $7.99 a month, with cancellation available at any time. Netflix ranges in cost, with streaming available for new members for $7.99 a month. Current DVD/Blu-ray subscriber accounts can add a streaming plan for $4.99 a month for limited streaming, and $7.99 for unlimited streaming to multiple devices.

When comparing these costs, Amazon's service is about $16 cheaper than HuluPlus or Netflix and adds the free 2-day shipping feature for many products on the website, which is why many consumers go for their service. The shipping charges saved alone can make sense for many individuals who shop online often.

It is best for anyone who wants to subscribe to one or several of these services to check out that particular provider's content selection to determine if the monthly cost justifies the content you will be able to stream and watch.

Two other options you might consider are HBO GO, which is a streaming video service available to HBO cable or satellite package subscribers, and Vudu.com. Vudu is another online movie rental and purchase site which offers standard and hi-definition movies you can rent or download. I tested out Vudu and it works well with the Dolphin Browser and Adobe Flash installed on a Kindle Fire HD. Vudu does not work on the Silk Browser because it does not have Flash.

How to Watch YouTube Videos

The YouTube app is finally available on the Kindle Fire HD. This app is free in the Amazon Appstore, so download it, sign into your account, and begin watching all the YouTube videos you want to watch.

Another way to watch the videos is through the browser. You can view YouTube videos on your Kindle Fire HD. YouTube videos should play on the standard Silk browser that your Fire HD uses for web browsing.

How to Download YouTube Videos onto Your KFHD

While Amazon offers a lot of great content in terms of videos, you may want to really stock up on videos, say if you are going on a trip and need something to stay entertained while traveling.

To download YouTube videos to the Kindle Fire HD, you can use an app called TubeMate, which is not found at Amazon Appstore. Here's how to install and use the app:

1. Go to the Web browser on your Kindle Fire HD and enter tubemate.net in the bar at the top.
2. Once at TubeMate.net, tap on "Download (Handster)" button.
3. At the next screen hold down on the blue "Download" button you see. You may need to enlarge your web screen display to make the button larger, and then press down on it.
4. A box will pop up. Tap on "Open." The Tubemate download will begin.
5. Once completed, the Tubemate app will be in your notifications area. Tap on the TubeMate download there, and then tap on "Install" at the bottom of the next screen.
6. Tap on "Open" button at the bottom of next screen to open TubeMate.
7. When a pop-up box appears, you can tap on the checkbox next to "I don't want to see it anymore" and then tap the "Close" button.
8. You'll now be able to search for YouTube videos to watch. Once they're playing you can tap on the green arrow at the bottom of your screen to download the video to your device. Videos can be downloaded as

1280x720 since the Kindle Fire HD is a "high-end device."

9. The video will be downloaded and will show up in your notifications area. You can also see all the videos you download from the TubeMate app while in TubeMate. Just click on the folder icon at the lower right-hand area of the screen.

There's much more you can do with the app in terms of settings, but these are the basics to download YouTube videos for future viewing on your Kindle Fire HD.

How to Take a Screenshot

Here's a neat trick with your Kindle Fire HD. You can easily take a screenshot photo of whatever is currently on your device screen. This may be helpful for showing others a particular app or settings area of your device, or many other reasons for showing off the screen. Here's how to do it:

1. Make sure you have the particular screen displaying on your Kindle Fire HD that you want to take a screenshot of.
2. Hold down the Power and Volume down buttons.
3. The screen will flash and make a sound indicating a picture was taken. The screenshot will briefly show up on your screen, and then will be stored in your "Photos" area of the device.

You can then move these to another device via the USB connection to a computer or laptop, and upload them or store them in your Cloud if you'd prefer.

How to use the Camera

You can take both pictures and video with the camera on the KFHD. These pictures can be saved to the device or upload automatically to Cloud Drive storage. The great news is, photos and videos you take with your KFHD do not count toward your totally Cloud Drive Storage.

1. To upload photos and videos to Cloud Diver automatically:
2. Tap "Photos" on the "Home" screen.
3. Swipe from the left edge of the screen, and tap "Settings."
4. Under "Auto-Save," tap the slider next to "Photos" and "Videos" to enable the automatic upload.

To take a picture or video complete the following steps:

1. Tap the "Camera" icon from the "Home" screen.
2. Press the shutter, or tap the "Video" icon to switch to video and press record.

Tip: To open the Camera app from the lock screen, simply swipe from the bottom right corner of the screen.

Tip: Press and hold the shutter to capture images rapidly.

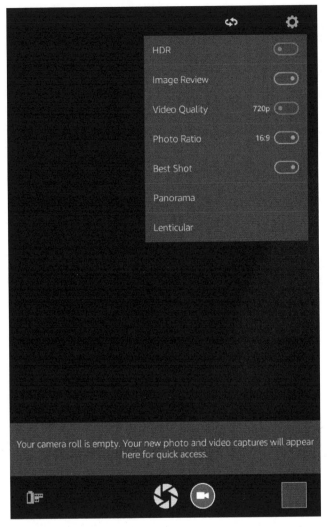

You can tap the following camera settings to turn them on or off.

- HDR
- Image Review
- Video Quality (supported devices only)
- Photo Ratio (supported devices only)
- Best Shot (supported devices only)
- Panorama
- Lenticular

Camera Roll

The camera app on the KFHD allows you to edit images directly on the screen, simply by selecting a photo you want to alter, and then using the tools available to remove red eye, crop the image as a whole or change the look of the image to black and white or sepia tones.

You can also edit images you did not take with the device, which can be great for future use. You may also delete images the second you take them, or roll through the collection to see what can stay and what can go.

If you are in a zone, start taking pictures like crazy and analyze them later to determine which ones stay – and become part of the collection – and which ones go.

How to Print from KFHD

The Kindle Fire HD tablet supports printing documents, spreadsheets, presentations, photos, and emails to your home or office's wireless printer without any hassle. Simply choose the document, image or email you would like to print, and select "Print" from the menu button that is available at the top of the document. The printer must be configured as an option – or at least obtainable through your Bluetooth or Wi-Fi capabilities.

How to Create Collections

Depending on which device you purchase, you will be allotted a certain amount of memory on your hard drive. With that space you can download apps, music, movies, eBooks, documents and peripherals in abundance, leaving them directly on the device for easy access. Keep in mind that if they are stored on your device, and not syncing through your Cloud Collections, that is going to be the only place you can find that data, which is perfectly fine should you want to keep it that way.

You are also able to take advantage of Amazon's amazing Cloud capabilities, so the space on your device is not devoured by entertainment. Although the amount of memory used on the device should not affect its operation – as the dual core processor is still lightning fast – it does make sense to keep your items in the Cloud – specifically for back-up purposes. This way, if anything happens to your KFHD, you have everything stored remotely so you can download it again with ease, or at the very access it in an emergency.

Everything you purchase from Amazon is automatically stored in their Cloud, and can be accessed from any device, at any time, as long as you have an Internet connection. You can also organize your content library into Collections like "Favorite Books" and "Sports Apps" that are synchronized with your other Kindle devices and reading apps, so you will always be on the same page – no matter where you are accessing your material from.

What's more is that the new KFHD has a new 1-Tap Archive. This option frees up space on your Kindle Fire HD by identifying items that have not been used recently. Those items will be quickly moved to your Cloud for later retrieval, simply by tapping the 1-tap option.

At all times, no matter what you are downloading to your device, the KFHD ensures that is it is transferred through optimization download, so your current use of the device is not affected by the activity happening in the background.

To create a collection complete the following:

1. From a content category tap "Library," swipe from the left edge of the screen, and tap "Collections."
2. From your "Collections" page, tap the + icon. Enter a name for the collection, and tap "Create."
3. Tap the titles you want to include in your collection, and then tap "Add."

Note: To remove an item from a collection, press and hold the item, tap the three vertical dots icon in the top right, and tap "Remove from this collection."

How to Download Prime Instant Videos

First things first: When you purchase a new KFHD, you will automatically receive a free 30-day trial of Amazon Prime. This means you can order anything you desire from Amazon, and ship it two-day without any extra cost. In addition, you receive access to the Amazon Prime Instant videos, books, music, and more simply by being a member!

Prime members enjoy commercial-free, unlimited streaming of thousands of popular movies and TV shows at no extra cost. Simply find the movie or series you would like to view, and tap on its icon to begin the download.

In addition, you can borrow any title from the Kindle Owners' Lending Library for free, and read one free book a month – or as they desire thereafter – without the pressure of due dates, late fees or charges of any kind. There are literally hundreds of different titles waiting to be checked out for free using this service.

Finally – and the coolest feature by far – is that KFHD owners can download Prime Instant Video movies and television shows and watch them offline! This means you do not have to have Internet access to stream your favorite release on an airplane, train or even in your car. Prime Instant Video is the only U.S. online video subscription streaming service that offers offline viewing, and it's included at no additional cost.

How to use Second Screen

Much like Apple has Airplay, which allows you to turn your iPad into a remote for your big screen with an Apple TV streaming device, Kindle Fire HD has followed suit by turning your tablet into an entertainment hub that "Flings" content onto a larger screen, to view with a group. This content can be pictures, videos, movies, television programming or even your email inbox.

All you need is the KFHD, an Amazon Fire TV or a Fire TV Stick. The best part is, you can continue to work on your tablet while the television displays alternate content, so you can check emails or look for content on the web as you desire, while enjoying the programming remotely.

Second Screen allows your TV to act as the primary viewing screen, while you use your tablet in companion mode. The tablet can be the remote control, or you can use it for X-ray features to learn more about what you're watching. In addition, you can browse the web, check your email, and many other things while you're using Second Screen.

To use Second Screen, ensure both devices are turned on.

1. From your Fire tablet, tap Videos, and then Store. Find the movie or show you want to watch.
2. From the video's details, tap the Second Screen icon.
3. Select the Second Screen device you want to send the movie or TV show to, and the video will load and begin playing on your device.
4. When you're finished watching, tap the Second Screen icon and select your Fire tablet to end the playback on your connected device.

Other Helpful Kindle Fire HD Features

There are many interesting features available for the Kindle devices. Below are several of these features.

VoiceView

VoiceView on your Kindle Fire HD allows you to use Text-to-Speech to read and interaction with books. The Text-to-Speech option automatically reads books and turns pages for you.

← VoiceView

VoiceView
Provides spoken feedback when you touch items on the screen. To disable
VoiceView, select Off and then double tap anywhere on the screen.

Reading Speed
3 (Default)

VoiceView Volume
Match device volume

Feedback Tone Volume
Match device volume

Key Echo
characters

Punctuation Level
some

VoiceView Tutorial

Go to Text to Speech

There are two modes for VoiceView – Continuous and non-
continuous. The continuous mode reads all the pages in a
book, and the non-continuous reads a page, character, or word
on the page.

How to use VoiceView

Note: When you are in VoiceView, you will tap once to select and item, and then double tap to select that item.

To turn VoiceView on:

1. Swipe down from the top of the screen.
2. Tap "Settings."
3. Tap "Accessibility."
4. Tap "VoiceView" to turn the feature on.

Start reading – Swipe down from the top of the page with two fingers when the reading toolbar is closed. Text-to-Speech stars reading the book and turns the pages automatically.

Switch from continuous to non-continuous – Simply tap the screen to switch from reading continuously to reading one page at a time. VoiceView can also be adjusted to read one word, line, or character at a time depending on what suits you best.

Note: Depending on the content being read, some reading level options may not be available.

Show Reading Toolbar – While inside a book, tap the screen, then double-tap the screen to show the reading toolbar.

Change Reading Voice – With the reading toolbar open, swipe down from the top of the screen with two fingers to open Quick Actions, select "Settings." From "Settings," select "Keyboard & Language," and then select "Text-to-Speech."

To turn off VoiceView:

1. Swipe down from the top of the screen open "Quick Settings."
2. Tap "Settings," then double-tap the screen to open the "Settings" menu.

3. Tap "Accessibility," then double-tap the screen to open the "Accessibility" menu.
4. Tap "VoiceView," then double-tap the screen.
5. Next to VoiceView Reader, double tap the switch to turn it of.
6. Tap Continue and confirm.

X-ray Features

The Kindle Fire HD has expanded its X-ray technology to include more than just books. Initially, the feature was available to allow readers to look up the meaning of a word by simply tapping on it, or to review the when, where, what and why of an event, place or occasion.

That technology has been developed for use during movies so you can check on an actor's name, biography, other roles and scenes without leaving the movie. It delivers the ever-popular IMDb app information within the movie. To access this feature on a movie that offers X-ray, all you need to do is tap the screen during a scene and it will pop-up information such as which actors and actresses are appearing and more!

In addition to regular books, X-ray is now available for textbooks, providing the user with Wikipedia and YouTube glossary references to enhance the learning experience, without leaving the page.

X-ray for music is also available for Kindle devices. The words to X-ray enabled songs will scroll on the right-hand side of the screen as you hear them.

Whispersync for Books, Games, Movies, and Voice

Whispersync for Voice is cutting edge technology that allows you to toggle between reading a Kindle book and listening to its companion audiobook without losing your place. It will also remember your position, and keep your notes and bookmarks. Additionally, it will keep your place among multiple devices.

When used for games, movies and books, this technology will sync each device you are enjoying the entertainment on, placing you directly where you left off on the other.

Cloud Storage vs. Device Storage

Amazon has made technology more user friendly than ever before by allowing you to store any Amazon purchased content on their Cloud, instead of devour the allotted storage on the actual device.

Depending on the version you purchase, you may be limited to 16GB of device storage, which means any non-Amazon purchased content will start eating away at that space immediately. This can include any iTunes music, videos, movies, or television content you purchased through Apple. However, each and every piece of content you purchase through Amazon can be stored on their Cloud server for free, without any size restrictions. This virtual storage capability can be accessed from anywhere with an Internet connection, even if you do not have your Kindle Fire HD handy.

What You Can Store on Your Tablet

There is no limit to the digital files you can store on your tablet, including music, movies, apps, documents, contacts, eBooks, games, pictures and video. As long as it fits within your storage parameters, you can pack away files left and right until you are at capacity.

You can transfer images, content and technology to your Kindle Fire device from your laptop or desktop computer, camera, cell phone, or video camera and access it as often as you would like going forward. You can also transfer items from your tablet to USB jump drives, computers and storage devices effortlessly, as a backup precaution. Later on in this guidebook, there are instructions for moving files to and from your Kindle Fire HD and a PC or MAC computer.

The Kindle Fire HD 8 and above also features a microSD slot, so you can purchase one and begin using that for storage on your Kindle Fire HD.

Extra Storage Options

There are many free apps out there allowing you to store extra files online. These include Dropbox, which is a very popular app for file storage and sharing, but it will be limited to 2GB of storage for the free version. Google Drive will also let you store various files online for access on computers and devices. You may need to install an app to use Google Drive with your Kindle Fire HD.

Additionally, you can purchase special wireless devices to hold your files for access at home on a wireless network. The Kingston Wi-Drive is available at Amazon.com in 16GB, 32GB and 64GB sizes. It will hold photos, music, documents, videos, and other files, and will allow you to access them wirelessly on your Kindle Fire HD. These devices will allow other computers within your home or office network to share and stream the files in addition to your Kindle Fire HD.

There is also the Maxell AirStash Expandable Capacity Wireless Flash Drive, which is available in 6 gigabyte or 16 gigabyte sizes. It is more expensive than the Wi-Drive, but a smaller, more portable option for file sharing wirelessly on your Kindle, computers, and other devices. These items will include specific instructions to help you set them up easily with your home network and you can then use them to store and access files with the Kindle Fire HD.

Family Library

Family Library allows you to link tow Amazon accounts to share apps, games, Kindle books, audiobooks, and Prime Video streaming using your KFHD. Content from both accounts can be shared with two adult profiles and up to four child profiles.

When you enable Family Library shared content from linked accounts are available from the Amazon Cloud for your Fire tablet and other registered apps and compatible devices. You can filter the content to see only what you want to see on your device.

Note: Each profile that accesses shared content has its own settings for the shared content including furthest page read, application data, game progress and more.

To enable Family Library, both account holders must authorize each other to use credit cards used on each account for Amazon purchases. If you separate accounts, each adult has to wait 180 days to join a new household or link a new Amazon account to Family Library.

To enable Family Library complete the following:

1. Swipe down from the top of your screen and tap settings.
2. Tap "Profiles and Family Library."
3. Tap the Adult Profile to create a Family Library with, and tape Enable Sharing.
4. Both adults must agree to share payment methods and tap "Continue."
5. Select content types to share in the Family Library,
6. Allow the second adult to sign into Amazon from your Kindle Fire HD and Confirm that that want to enable content sharing. The second adult will also choose what content types to share.

Note: *Selecting a content type will share all current and future purchases in that category.*

Kindle Fire HD Tips and Tricks

While you probably have the basics down, there is some neat Kindle Fire HD tips and tricks to use to get the most out of your Amazon tablet.

Music and Videos

Although your KFHD will not support iTunes, it will allow you to drop and drag your own music and videos onto the device effortlessly. Simply attached the device to your computer or laptop, and drag the files you wish to appear on the KFHD accordingly. For music, the device supports MP3, AAC, FLAC and OGG filed. For video, the device supports H.264, MPEG4, Xvid and DivX videos up to 1080p.

In addition, Netflix and Pandora work beautifully on this device, which will allow you to stream unlimited movies, television and music with the appropriate subscriptions to each service. Both have a free trial, so you can experience their capabilities before settling into a monthly subscription service.

The high-resolution screen that is included with the KFHD provides an exceptional viewing experience for HD movies, and really brings your device to life while watching any form of entertainment. The onscreen clarity and vividness of the colors is unbelievable, and will enhance your viewing experience each time a high definition option is available.

Just as X-Ray is available for music – to help you learn all of the proper lyrics to your favorite songs, it is also available for movies! This feature allows you to get information on the actors, or even the backstories characters, simply by tapping on the feature button. Now you will never miss a single detail of a new show, or even an old favorite.

How to use Voice to Text with KFHD Keyboard

If you are typing an email or a message in Facebook or other messaging service, you can use voice to text to create the message.

To use this feature, simply press the microphone button to the left of the "," on the keyboard. Begin speaking. Double check the text, and then press send to sent the message.

How to Print from Kindle

If you own a printer that supports wireless printing, then you can print straight from your KFHD tablet.

Note: *Personal documents in the Kindle format cannot be printed.*

If your Fire Tablet doesn't recognize your printer, download a print plugin for your device from the Amazon appstore.

To print, ensure your printer is both on and connected to Wi-Fi, and then print the document using the following steps:

1. Tap the menu icon for the item you want to print, and then tap print.
2. Select your printer from the list. If you don't see your printer on the list, tap "All Printers" to search for nearby printers.
3. Select the number of copies to print. You can also tap "More options" to chose other things like Color Mode, Paper Size, and Orientation.
4. Tap Print.

How to use Send to Kindle Plugin for PC and Mac Web Browsers

The Docs area of your Kindle Fire HD tablet provides several ways to send documents over to your device. One of these ways is a feature you can use when online via a personal computer or laptop and you're browsing the web.

With the "Send to Kindle" feature, you can clip various web content such as articles or blog posts, and then have them automatically sent to your device to read later on.

1. You'll need to install a plugin for the web browser you use most, whether it is Google Chrome or Mozilla Firefox.
2. The plug-in should give you a small "K" icon for Kindle that shows up near the top of your web browser. You can click on this icon whenever you are on a webpage article you want to clip and send to your KFHD.

3. You'll be able to preview the item before it sends, and then click on "Send" from your web browser to send the formatted article to your device.

You can access all your "Send-to-Kindle" Docs by going to the "Docs" option on your Kindle's top menu and then tapping on the three lines up in the left corner of the screen to reveal a menu of options. Tap "My Send-to-Kindle Docs" to access your latest documents sent.

Note: *Keep in mind it may take several minutes for the document to arrive to your Kindle device. It will be sent via Wireless and could take some extra time to arrive. You can also try to speed up the delivery process on your Kindle tablet by tapping on "Settings" and then "Sync All Content."*

How to Opt out of Ads on Kindle

Some Kindle Fire HD owners may find the constant sponsored ads from Amazon on their device to be annoying. For a charge of $15, you can easily opt out of receiving the various sponsored ads from Amazon that show up on your Kindle Fire HD. You can do this by going to your Amazon.com account online and going to "Manage Your Device" to opt out of ads for the $15 charge.

How to Use the Kindle Fire as a Phone

A hidden gem of tips for your tablet is that you can turn it into a phone and make calls easily! Viber has a free app available at the Amazon Appstore called "Viber." The beauty of this app is that you can install it for free on your Kindle Fire HD and then use it to make phone calls (although calls may be limited to Canada and U.S.).

Once you install this app, you'll be asked to type in your phone number.

Note: You do have to have Viber installed on your phone device in order to use it on your tablet.

Once you have set up your account for Viber, use it to dial up a local number such as your home phone or someone's mobile phone to give it a try.

How to Conserve Battery Life

In addition to installing a good battery app such as Battery HD or GSam Battery Monitor, I recommend a few additional considerations and steps. These include the following:

- Shutting off Wi-Fi and Bluetooth when you are not using the device with a wireless network or another Bluetooth device.
- Dimming the screen display brightness.
- Allowing the device to recharge fully when plugged in, rather than trying to use it while charging.

How to Clean the Kindle Fire Display

It is important to limit the amount of smudges and marks that get onto your Kindle Fire HD display so it will provide good viewing and functionality over its lifetime. The best investment here is the screen protector. If you don't have a screen protector, then a microfiber cloth is essential. With a microfiber cloth you can wipe off any smudges or dust to keep your display looking great.

How to Factory Reset KFHD

You might want to factory reset your Kindle Fire HD if you are giving it away, or perhaps even if something happens and you want to start fresh with your device. The good news is it's fairly easy to reset your Kindle Fire HD to its factory settings.

Note: Resetting your tablet will remove all content and you will have to complete the setup again.

To do this, complete the follow steps:

1. Swipe down from the top of the screen.
2. Tap "Settings."
3. Tap "Device Options." Then tap "Reset to Factory Defaults."
4. Tap "Reset" to confirm.

Tip: All content saved in your Cloud will still remain in the cloud.

How to Backup and Restore KFHD

You can back up your Kindle Fire HD is case it is damaged or lost. If you do, you will be able to load all your content onto a new device. When you set up a new KFHD you have the option to set it up as a new device or restore the content from a backup.

To turn on automatic backup complete the following steps:

Swipe down from the top of the screen.

1. Tap "Settings."
2. Tap "Device Options."
3. Tap "Backup & Restore."
4. Tap the "Device Backup" switch to turn it on.

Note: Your KFHD will backup automatically every day when it is on standby and connected to Wi-Fi.

How to Sideload Apps

Sideloading is a fancy term for transferring media files from one device to another, usually from a USB drive, Bluetooth technology, or memory card. This ability allows you to transfer files effortlessly, which means you can have all of your images, documents, videos and music in one place, even if it is coming from someone else. Think of sideloading as something you have always done with your laptop or desktop computer, and expand that thought process to your new Kindle Fire HD. For the most part, the terminology here refers to a way to put apps onto your tablet that aren't necessarily available through the Amazon app store.

Sideloading Apps You Want for the KFHD

It is possible to transfer some of your favorite Android apps from your current device and sideload them onto your KFHD. There are two options that make this possible, and you are free to use a combination of both.

Using the APK Extractor App, you can copy an app from your current Android phone or device, and attach it to an email. Email it to yourself, and download it to your KFHD. Next, turn on "Apps from Unknown Sources" under Settings >Security, and tap on the downloaded app. The app will install effortless, and function normally.

You can also install the free ES File Explorer app that is available through the Amazon App Store. Tap Settings > Security > Advanced, then tap "On" to Allow Installation of Applications from Unknown Sources.

1. Google your app and search for the APK file.
2. Download the APK file to your computer.
3. Copy the APK file to the root (or a folder of your choice) on the Fire via a USB connection to your computer. After copied, disconnect the Fire from the computer by clicking Disconnect on the bottom of the Fire's screen and then unplug the USB cable.
4. Start ES File Explorer and select the APK file then select install when prompted.

If you do not own another Android device, side loading an app is trickier because the only way to get a legal copy of an APK file is from an app you have downloaded from the Google Play Store or other Android app store.

How to Add Google Play Store to Fire HD

While Amazon devices tend to mostly use apps from the Amazon apps store, the good news is you can also use apps from Google Play. Even better, there is a way to install the Google Play store right onto your device without having to root the tablet like in the past.

A word of caution though, when using any third party apps with your device, it is up to the tablet owner to decide if they trust the websites, file downloads and installations enough to add them to their tablet.

For those who are interested in adding Google Play Store onto the Fire HD, here are the step-by-step instructions:

1. Go to your Fire HD's Settings area and tap on "Security."
2. Tap on "Apps from Unknown Sources." You will receive a pop-up warning. Read this and make sure you are OK with the warning, then click OK to proceed.
3. Open the Silk Browser on your Fire HD. Search for "Google Play Store."
4. Go to Google Play Store and find ES File Explorer File Manager.
5. Copy the URL link on the Silk browser. You can bring up the option to Copy or Cut by tapping on the URL link at the top of your browser.
6. Go to the third party evozi website: http://apps.evozi.com/apk-downloader/
7. Tap on the entry area (under Package name or Google Play URL) to paste the Google Play URL link you copied.
8. Tap on the blue button for "Generate Download Link" and wait for a moment.
9. Tap on the green button that appears, "Click here to download..." You may receive a prompt at the bottom of your screen. Make sure you are OK with the warning and click "OK" to proceed.
10. Once it has downloaded you should see a pop up at the bottom of your device screen where you can tap on "Open." This will open the ES File Explorer app.
11. Tap on "Install" after reading through what the ES File Explorer app will have the ability to do with your device.
12. Now you will need to open Silk Browser again, but this time go to the link to download each of the files you'll need to install for Google Play. You can find all four of these files at the third party shared storage link: **https://onedrive.live.com/?cid=73036323a69e3cf1&id=730 36323A69E3CF1%211484&authkey=%21AlVXLFXAOWDeM 0Q**
13. Download each of the four files to your Fire HD, one by one by tapping on them, and proceeding through the pop-up warning at the bottom of your devices.

14. Exit Silk browser and open your ES File Explorer app.
15. Tap on the "Downloads" folder and you should see all of the Google Play files you downloaded.
16. Tap on "Google Account Manager" first and tap on "Install" on the pop-up. You may also have to tap "Install" a second time after reading through what the app can do on your device. (Note: You must install these Google apps in the specified order per these instructions.)
17. Tap on "Google Play Services" to install that app next and tap "Install" on the pop-up ad as well as the screen that follows it.
18. Tap on "Google Services Framework" to install that app next and tap "Install" on the pop-up ad as well as the screen that follows it.
19. Tap on "Google Play Store" to install that app next and tap "Install" on the pop-up ad as well as the screen that follows it.
20. Now go to your Fire HD home screen and you should see the Play Store app icon. Tap to open it.
21. You'll be prompted to either add an "Existing" account using your current login for Google Play Store, or to add a "New" account which you will sign up for. Now you can use the Google Play Store with your Fire HD.

Note: It's recommended that once you have Google Play Store installed and your account is active to go into the Google Play Store settings area on your device. Tap on the "Auto-update apps" and make sure "Do not auto-update apps" is selected.

How to Root a Kindle Fire Tablet

Rooting a Kindle Fire HD tablet is not something recommended for most users, so consider this an advanced tip and with a word of caution: rooting your tablet will void the warranty, and it may also cause glitches or issues if done improperly.

However, doing this in the past has allowed some users to access much more content and make certain adjustments to the tablet that couldn't be done before. For example, some users have been able to install the Google Play store on a KFHD tablet, allowing them a greater selection of apps and content to use on their tablet.

To root a Kindle Fire HD tablet you'll want to check out forums online such as XDA Developers, where users will discuss ways to do this. Normally it will involve downloading a large batch of .apk files and then installing them with the free ES File Explorer app from the Amazon App Store.

Once again, only root your device if you have a good idea what you're doing, and can handle the potential issues involved.

How to Get More Kindle Support

Looking for more answers on how to use your Kindle device? The Amazon website provides plenty of extra help for Kindle owners. There is a variety of Kindle Self-Service tools at the site including:

- Manage Your Kindle
- Manage Your Subscriptions
- 1-Click Payment Settings

- View Digital Purchases
- View Your Collections
- Kindle Help Forum

In particular, the Kindle Help Forum is a great resource for finding out answers to issues with your device that other members may have been able to resolve or address. There may also be new pieces of information from Amazon staff regarding future Kindle Fire HD updates there. To access these help areas and more visit the Kindle Support site.

How to get free and cheap eBooks for your Kindle Devices

There are plenty of free and cheap eBooks to be had for your new Kindle. Below is a list with links provided to different places you can visit online to find free or low-priced content for your device.

- Amazon's Kindle Store. On the right side of the page, there is a list of the top Paid and Free books for the day. Click on that list, and you will have access to the top free books of the day. http://www.amazon.com/gp/bestsellers/digital-text
- Amazon Kindle Owners Lending Library (for Amazon Prime Subscribers or Kindle Unlimited Subscribers) http://www.amazon.com/gp/feature.html?ie=UTF8&docId=1000739811
- Many Books - http://manybooks.net/
- Books on the Knob - http://blog.booksontheknob.org/
- Daily Cheap Reads - http://dailycheapreads.com/category/free/
- e-Reader Café - http://www.thee-Readercafe.com/

- Free Book Dude - http://www.freebookdude.com/search/label/Kindle?max-results=5
- Your Daily eBooks - http://www.yourdailyebooks.com/category/free-kindle-books/
- Bookbub – https://www.bookbub.com
- Freebooksy – http://www.freebooksy.com

Tip: You may also want to check with your local library. Many libraries currently offer eBook check out privileges for patrons to borrow various eBooks on Kindle devices.

Recommended Apps for Kindle Fire HD Owners

There are thousands of apps out there, but I recommend the following ones as some of the best basic apps you can get on your device. These cover the categories of news, productivity, utilities, and much more to help upgrade your tablet! The majority of these are available from the Amazon Appstore, but some are available from third party sites.

Candy Crush Saga – Finally this incredibly popular game from King is available for the Kindle Fire! Hooray for Candy Crush lovers everywhere. You can crush candy to heart's content on your Kindle Fire devices simply by downloading this game for free from the Amazon app store. Be sure you are careful about how much you spend in in app purchases.

Angry Birds Free – This is the go to game that most people love to play. It is a great time-killer to have on your Kindle Fire HD, and great for the kids to play. It features a slingshot you use to fling birds across the screen in an attempt to destroy various structures and enemies for points. A very addictive and fun game, so be careful! There's also Angry Birds Seasons Free and Angry Birds Space Free for those who want to try different versions of the game.

Battery HD – This is a great app for monitoring the levels of your Kindle Fire HD's remaining battery power. It will give you various displays including info on how much time you have left for viewing movies or videos, browsing the internet with Wi-Fi, reading books or more. A great app to get to make sure you conserve battery power and know when to charge back up! An alternate battery app to check out is called GSam Battery Monitor, which will tell you which apps might be using the most battery power on your device.

Calculator Plus Free – The Kindle Fire HD does not include a calculator as part of its features, although many other tablets do. Calculator Plus Free is currently the most reviewed, and highest rated of the free calculator apps at the Amazon Appstore. An alternate app to this is called Calculator and costs 0.99 cents.

Dropbox or SugarSync – These apps offer you more cloud storage than what you get with the free Amazon storage. They also allow for easier movement, streaming and sharing of files between your devices.

ES File Explorer – This is hands down one of the best apps to install on your Kindle Fire HD to really unlock and unleash more capabilities. Among those capabilities is the camera functionality we covered above, as well as the ability to manage all the files and folders on your device.

Facebook app – It is tough to find the Facebook app at the Amazon App Store, however you can access it at the link on the app name here.

YouTube – the YouTube app is a free download from Amazon for the KFHD, and it allows you to watch all your favorite YouTube videos from the app instead of using a the browser.

Hulu Plus – Hulu Plus is an online subscription service that allows its users to enjoy on demand access to television shows, movies, webisodes, news, trailers, clips, and behind the scenes footage for free from networks and studios, thanks to ad support. Many people opt for this service as an alternative to Netflix due to its variety of available television shows, movies and other entertainment.

imo Instant Messenger – Use this free app to connect with friends, family and colleagues across multiple instant messenger accounts. The app will worth with AIM, MSN, Yahoo, Skype, and much more!

OfficeSuite Professional 6 – While QuickOffice is a nice app for $15, there is also a free app called OfficeSuite Professional 6. This app is compatible with MS office files. It also allows you create, edit, view or save the various Office files, meaning more productivity on the road when you don't have access to your computer or laptop.

Netflix – If you currently have a paid Netflix account to enjoy streaming movies, you'll want to get this app. This will allow you to watch all of the same streaming Netflix movies you can watch on compatible Blu-ray players, computers, and other internet devices. A must-have for those with the Netflix subscription and a Kindle Fire HD who want to enjoy more movies than what Amazon has.

PicShop Lite Photo Editor – An alternate option in terms of camera apps is called PicShop Lite Photo Editor, also available at Amazon App Store. There are both free and paid versions of this app. The free version is very similar to the camera app discussed earlier in this guidebook, which can be accessed with ES File Explorer.

Pandora – Pandora is an alternate music app to Spotify (mentioned below). It can be used to play music based on radio stations created from your personal music preferences. For example, choose the artist Barbara Streisand, or Guns N' Roses, and it will create a radio station with music from the same genres as the original artist. This is a great free or paid app for streaming music radio style.

SplashTop Remote Desktop – Use this paid app to control your desktop from a remote location, such as while away on travel. Your desktop or laptop computer will need to be on to do so, and you'll have to install the SplashTop software on the device you want to control. Still, for $4.99 this is a great item for many people who want access to their home computer while on the road, or even from inside their home.

Spotify – Spotify is an online music streaming service that can be accessed by anyone who has a Facebook account. Once you register your account, you can listen to unlimited music for six months, thanks to its radio style sponsored advertising. Music can be browsed by artist, song title, album title, genre or playlist. After the trial period, there is a ten-hour listening limit per month, divided into two and one half hours per week for unpaid subscriptions. An unlimited subscription is available, and provides access to music without advertisements or time limits. A premium subscription is available that provides the unlimited access, no commercials or time limits and a higher bit rate of streaming, combined with offline access and a mobile app accessory.

textPlus – Created by GogiiInc, this app allows you to send texts for free to people around the world who also have the textPlus app. Not only that, it will work for sending out text messages to people in Canada and the United States who don't have the app. The textPlus app is available in both free and paid versions.

TubeMate – A third party app not in the Amazon appstore, this will allow you to watch and download YouTube videos on your Kindle Fire HD. A great way to get videos to watch at a later time, such as on a flight or during travel, so you don't have to worry about having a wireless connection to watch them! This book provided detailed instructions in a previous section to help you get going with this one.

Tune In Radio – A great free app that allows you to stream local and national radio stations on your Kindle Fire HD. Listen to your favorite local radio station while doing other activities on the Kindle. It also features other categories such as sports, talk, news, and podcast programs to select from.

As noted, there are tons and tons of apps being sold with new apps created daily. Those listed above are just several options you can consider to really upgrade your Kindle Fire HD for entertainment, productivity and more.

Apps not Available from the Amazon App Store

Since technology is still divided in it use, as it has been for decades, some apps are simply not compatible with the KFHD. Just like Apple does not promote Flash, this device has a few apps that are not optimized for its use. It is their loss, really.

- Instagram: All of those square, filtered pictures you have enjoyed up to date are going to have to come from your smartphone, because the KFHD does not support the app.
- Google Chrome & Mozilla Firefox: The Kindle Fire HD comes with "Silk" as its provided browser, and you will not be able to override it with a preference of your own.
- Google Drive: If you count on Google Drive to store documents you need throughout the day, you may want to consider switching to Amazon's Cloud for these purposes, as you will not be able to access your library from your Kindle.

There are also a number of Android widgets that are not compatible with the Kindle Fires. Since the number of widgets available is practically innumerable – and the varying options that people use are almost as high in quantity – it would be impossible to list all of them here. Just keep in mind that some of your widgets may not make the cut, but you should be able to find an Amazon friendly alternative.

If you really want these apps, you can attempt to sideload them onto your Kindle device, per the instructions in this book, but keep in mind the legal issues involved with sideloading apps.

Troubleshooting Kindle Fire HD

While using your Kindle Fire HD, you may run into some minor issues with it. These can be frustrating, and the following sections have some things to try when you run into minor difficulties.

Screen Frozen or Device Unresponsive

The first thing to try if your screen is frozen or unresponsive is to restart your tablet. Simply press and hold the power button for 40 seconds, and your device should restart. If it does not restart, release the power button and press it again to turn your tablet back on.

Purchased or Downloaded Content not Appearing

If content you have purchased or downloaded to your Kindle Fire HD does not appear you can try out the following things.

- Verify your device is registered to the correct account. Swipe down from the top of the screen, and tap "Settings." Then tap "My Account." If the wrong account is listed, you can tap on Deregister and then tap it again to confirm. After that, you can tap Register to register your tablet to the correct Amazon account.
- Verify that you are in the correct household profile by swiping down from the top of the screen and tapping on the

profile icon in the upper right of the Quick Settings menu. Tap the correct profile.

- If your device is on the correct profile and registered to the correct account, then double check to make sure it is connected to the Wi-Fi. If it is, swipe down from the top of the screen and tap "Sync Device."

Battery Doesn't Charge

If your KFHD does not charge be sure you are using the power adapter and micro-USB cord that came with the device to charge it. Also, use a power outlet to charge the device instead of a USB port. Make sure that the micro-USB cord is connected to your power adapter and your tablet.

If your device still won't charge after checking those issues, then try the following steps:

1. Unplug the power adapter and the micro-USB cable from your device, and then reconnect them.
2. Insert the power adaptor into a power outlet.
3. If your device doesn't indicate it is charging, unplug the power adapter. Press and hold the Power button for 40 seconds to restart the device.
4. After you restart your tablet, plug the power adapter and micro-USB cable into the device and charge for at least one hour.

Note: If your device sound is turned on, you will hear a confirmation that the battery is charging.

Can't Connect to Wi-Fi

You may find that your KFHD is unable to connect to Wi-Fi. If this happens, be sure to check these items first.

- Ensure that other devices in your home can connect to the network. If nothing connects, contact your Internet Service Provider for additional help.
- Make sure that Airplane Mode is off. Swipe down from the top of the screen. The Airplane Mode icon should be gray with a line through it. If it's not gray, you can tap the icon to turn it on.
- Make sure you know the correct Wi-Fi password.
- Make sure your KFHD has the latest software version. To install the latest software you can download and transfer the software update to your device via USB.

If all of those things are okay, try the following actions:

- Restart your tablet's Wi-Fi connection. Swipe down from the top of the screen and tap Wi-Fi. Turn the switch next to Wi-Fi off. Once the Wi-Fi connection is turned off, tap the switch to turn it back on.
- Restart your tablet. Press and hold the Power button for 40 seconds or until the device restarts automatically.
- Move closer to your router.
- Restart your router and modem.

If you still cannot connect to the Wi-Fi, you can contact your Internet service provider for more help.

Can't Connect to Bluetooth Devices

You may find that you are unable to connect to your Bluetooth devices. If this happens, there are a few things to check before you begin troubleshooting.

- Confirm that your Bluetooth accessory is compatible with your tablet.
- Turn on Bluetooth pairing on your supported devices.
- Verify that the accessory is within range of your Kindle Fire HD. You can't pair your tablet with your Bluetooth accessory if they are too far apart.

After checking all those things, try the following:

1. Swipe down from the top of the screen and tap Bluetooth.
2. Tap the switch next to Bluetooth to turn on. The switch will turn.
3. On the device you want to pair with your tablet, make sure that Bluetooth is turned on so that the device is discoverable.
4. On your tablet, tap Pair a Bluetooth Device. A list of available Bluetooth devices will appear.
5. Tap the Bluetooth accessory you wish to pair your tablet, and follow any additional pairing instructions.

If these steps do not work, restart your Kindle Fire HD, and attempt to pair the devices again.

Accidentally Purchased Content

You may have accidentally purchased content using your Kindle Fire HD. If so, you can get some help by trying the following things.

Tip: Turn on parental controls to prevent others from making accidental purchases on your tablet.

Accidentally purchased books:

If you notice you've accidentally purchased a book, you may be able to request a refund within seven days of purchase through the Manage Your Content and Devices page or by contacting Customer Service.

1. Go to Manage Your Content and Devices on Amazon.com and locate the book you want to return.
2. Next to the title, click the Actions button, and then click Return for refund.

Accidental purchases from Amazon Video:

You can cancel purchases from the Amazon Video store within 24 hours of purchase if you have not attempted to stream or download the accidentally purchased video. For more information, go to Cancel an Accidental Amazon Video Order.

Note: You cannot return accidentally purchased music.

Forgot Lock Screen Password or PIN

If you set a lock screen password or PIN, and you forget it, you can reset it from the lock screen on your device.

1. Enter the wrong password or PIN five times. After the fifth incorrect attempt, a notification will appear with options to wait 30 seconds, reset your PIN, or factory reset your device.
2. Tap Reset Your PIN.
3. Enter your Amazon account password, and then tap Continue.
4. Enter your new PIN or Password, and then tap Finish.

Another option is to change your device's lock screen password or PIN directly from the Manage Your Content and Devices page on amazon.com.

Accessories to Consider for Fire HD Tablets

As with any great tech device, there are always a good variety of accessories available to help enhance the gadget's features, as well as the positive and complementary functionality that they deliver. Fire HD accessories range from a good protective or multi-functional case all the way up to streaming media devices for enjoying your tablet's content on the big screen television!

Cases

Available for purchase with the Kindle Fire HD devices are several different cases help to protect and bring a little flair to your device. Some of these cases help stand up the tablet for flat surface viewing, so you don't have to hold it during a movie or presentation. Amazon offers a variety of different cases, which range in price and material used. These include the Incipio Clario Folio case with a translucent back and snap-on tab to keep the case securely shut while on the go.

In addition, there are stylish leather cases, and more heavy-duty "Defense" cases – that will envelope your device into safety so even an inadvertent drop will not harm your favorite device. Also, for the daintier owner, you may be able to purchase design emblazoned slim sleeve cases, so you can carry your Kindle Fire device in style.

Stylus

Sometimes it just makes more sense to have a "pen" when you are operating your device, especially if you are in a meeting or presentation during its use. Purchasing a stylus pen to control the device, while tapping apps, adding content and viewing material is a mere $10 away (or less). You may even find a bundle of several different colored stylus pens for purchase at this price point.

If you choose to turn your entire tablet into an interactive device, you may be able to find a bundle package, which includes a stylus and case. Some of these allow for you to hold the device with a built in elastic strap, and includes a built-in Stylus/Pen Combo. Some of these cases may also include built-in ID, credit card, and SD cardholders for your convenience.

Screen Protector

Outside of a case for your little beauty, a screen protector is probably the next most essential accessory to purchase. It will help prevent accidental or inadvertent scratches from appearing on the screen, should you happen to slide it into your purse, briefcase or backpack for a quick transport. Likewise, you never know when something sharp or pointed will come in contact with your device, so it is better to be safe than sorry.

Not only will these protect screen from harm, they also cut down on fingerprints and glare, so you can enjoy your device at any time, without feeling like it needs a good wipe down all the time. Make sure to choose a reputable brand such as NuPro, Moshi or Tech Armor so you can have confidence that your device is well protected.

Micro SD Storage Card(s)

Since the latest Fire HD tablet devices have included on-board storage, it makes perfect sense to pick up at least one or more Micro SD storage cards. These will allow you to store extra content such as photos, music, videos or other files. Keep in mind you also have free Amazon Cloud storage, but these storage cards can let you swap in and out different media content or files as needed when you're on the go.

Depending on which model of Fire HD tablet you own, you will be able to expand to a total 128 gigabytes of extra storage with a Micro SD card. You can buy cards as small as 16GB or as large as the 128GB for your tablet. Trusted brands of Micro SD storage cards include Kingston, SanDisk and Samsung.

Bluetooth Keyboard

For some users, it's essential to have a more regular keyboard in addition to the on-board one that gets tapped on. It can save your table from being pressed on too much and make it easier for typing for many individuals. For this reason, wireless Bluetooth keyboards have become incredibly popular for using as accessories with tablets, including the Fire HD.

You can purchase a Bluetooth keyboard alone (such as AmazonBasics), or may find some that are offered built into a travel/protective case. An external keyboard is great for typing long emails and reports or even for creating presentations on the go. Basically, you receive the benefits of a real-sized keyboard, with the functionality of a tablet!

Bluetooth Headphones

Much like your regular headphones or ear buds, Bluetooth headphones allow you to enjoy the sound of music, movies or audio books, without physically connecting the headphones themselves into the device. This is great if you would like to keep your device tucked away, or do not want to be tethered to it as you sit at your desk, perhaps, so there is no chance of you sliding your chair across your office, and dangerously dragging the device with you. This is perfect for at home use too, if you are working around the house or garden, cleaning or preparing meals, as you can listen to your favorite audio items while you move about freely. As always, make sure to check with a retailer for compatibility with your particular device.

Headphones or Earbuds

If you are sitting still, and have the device in front of you, say on an airplane or train while watching a movie, your regular headphones will connect to your device with ease, allowing you to listen without interruption. At the current time, there are a lot more standard headphone or earbud varieties available on the market compared to Bluetooth counterparts. Some of the popular name brands include Bose, Sony and Beats.

Bluetooth Speakers

Much like the Bluetooth headphones, a wireless Bluetooth speaker will allow you to connect your music to a speaker that can be moved anywhere in your home or outside, so you can entertain literally wherever you are. You can take it to the beach, to a picnic, or simply allow it to ride with you on road trips, so you can access it in your hotel room. This incredibly smart device works the same way all Bluetooth capable devices do.

With a Bluetooth speaker, all you have to do is turn it on and allow your tablet to recognize it, before delving into your entire musical library or Pandora, so you are never without tunes – no matter where you are. One particular model we highly recommend is the JBL Flip speaker, which has a great price, great sound and convenient portability. It even allows some smartphone users to use the speaker as a speakerphone for phone calls.

Amazon Echo

The Amazon Echo is an innovative speaker device, which makes an excellent companion for your tablet. Echo takes the wireless Bluetooth speaker concept a step further. While you can stream music to it wirelessly over your Fire tablet's Bluetooth connection, if you're an Amazon Prime member you can also access millions of songs through Amazon's free digital music library and play those through the speaker without Bluetooth. Not only that, it provides spoken feedback and interactions including answers to questions or requests.

Simply download the Echo app to your Fire HD and connect the Echo to your Wi-Fi network. From there you can enjoy music on the Echo, but you can also hear spoken information such as weather updates for your region or other locations, news flash updates, sports scores and team schedule info, and so much more. Use the app on your Fire tablet to control and view your latest requests, modify Echo settings, set up music playlists and more.

Fire TV or Fire TV Stick

A great way to really enjoy your tablet is by also purchasing the Fire TV or Fire TV Stick to go with it. These devices allow you to watch streaming media on its own, but coupled with your Fire HD tablet, they allow for so much more. The tablet can stream content to the television screen or even mirror your Fire HD screen display for a much larger perspective. Imagine surfing the web via your tablet and seeing it presented on your large screen HDTV. In addition, a nifty app can be downloaded for your tablet, turning it into a touchscreen remote to control the Fire TV or Fire TV Stick!

Conclusion

The Kindle Fire HD contains a number of great features and exciting options for tablet users. Not only is a lightweight and beautiful device, but also its functionality has surpassed a number of tablets on the market, and is available at a lesser price point. Once you see the amazing screen, and how the colors come to life during movies and videos, you will wonder how you ever enjoyed your favorite television shows before.

The whole device allows you to access its features without getting a headache, as the flow of its design, and its amazing functionality will walk you through the lineaments without issue.

In a world of advancing technology, tablets are going to continue to upgrade and become newer with each step of the process. So far, the evolution of the Kindle devices that led up to the HD has nailed every segment of the market, allowing their clients to enjoy the benefits of Amazon actually listening to their feedback from previous iterations of the same device.

Take the time to discover which part of the KFHD works for you, and the only decision you will have to make after that is what size screen works best for you. The choice is yours, and so are the amazing accessory options that will allow you to turn your Kindle Fire HD into a personal expression of yourself - by day or night. All you need is a quick case change to take you from business to creative in a matter of seconds, so enjoy the versatility and the design at every turn. That is exactly what they are there for!

More Books by Shelby Johnson

How to Get Rid of Cable TV & Save Money: Watch Digital TV & Live Stream Online Media

Chromebook User Manual: Guide for Chrome OS Apps, Tips & Tricks!

Chromecast Dongle User Manual: Guide to Stream to Your TV (w/Extra Tips & Tricks!)

Google Nexus 7 User's Manual: Tablet Guide Book with Tips & Tricks!

Samsung Galaxy S5 User Manual: Tips & Tricks Guide for Your Phone!

Samsung Galaxy Tab 4 User Manual: Tips & Tricks Guide for Your Tablet!

Amazon Fire TV User Manual: Guide to Unleash Your Streaming Media Device

Roku User Manual Guide: Private Channels List, Tips & Tricks

Facebook for Beginners: Navigating the Social Network

iPhone 6 User's Manual: Tips & Tricks to Unleash the Power of Your Smartphone! (includes iOS 8)

iPhone 5 (5C & 5S) User's Manual: Tips and Tricks to Unleash the Power of Your Smartphone!

Apple TV User's Guide: Streaming Media Manual with Tips & Tricks

Yosemite OS X Manual: Your Tips & Tricks Guide Book

iPad Mini User's Guide: Simple Tips and Tricks to Unleash the Power of your Tablet!

Kindle Fire HDX & HD User's Guide Book: Unleash the Power of Your Tablet!

Kindle Paperwhite User's Manual: Guide to Enjoying your E-reader!

Made in the USA
Middletown, DE
17 December 2015